Enid Blyton™

TOYLAND™

Mr Plod
Activity Book

Collins

An Imprint of HarperCollinsPublishers

First published in Great Britain by HarperCollins Publishers Ltd in 1998

1 3 5 7 9 10 8 6 4 2

ISBN: 0 00 136097 3

Cover design and illustrations by County Studio

Printed and bound in Italy

WHAT'S WRONG?

Something is wrong with Noddy and each of his friends. Can you help Mr Plod to spot what it is?

Mr Plod needs these things to do his job. Can you find the odd one out in each row?

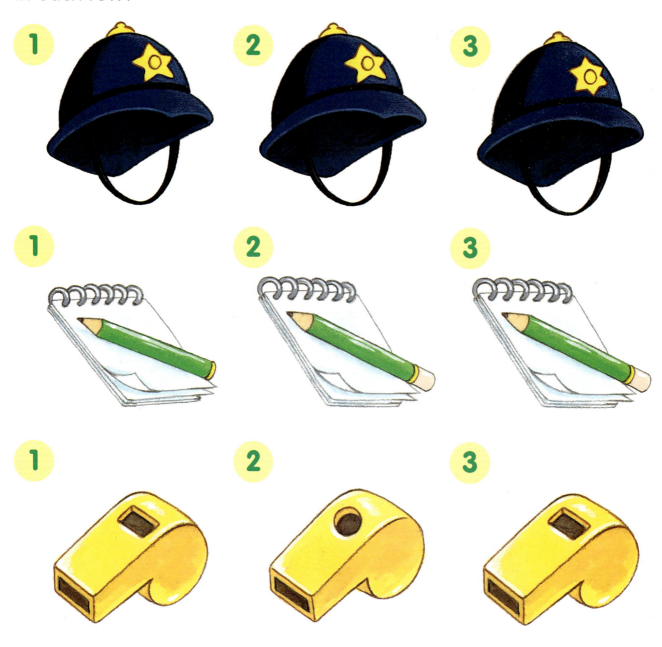

THE DARK WOOD

Mr Plod has been chasing the goblins through the Dark Wood and now he has got lost! Can you show him how to get back to Toy Town?

SPOT THE DIFFERENCE

Mr Plod is chasing the goblins again!

Can you find eight differences between these two pictures?

WHO STOLE THE FISH?

Someone has stolen the delicious, plump fish Miss Pink Cat bought for her supper. Help Mr Plod to find the thief.

Here are some clues:

1 **The thief is not the tallest or shortest here.**

2 **The thief does not wear a bow tie.**

3 **The thief does not wear a white jacket.**

MEMORY GAME

Sly and Gobbo are stealing again! Mr Plod has spotted them, but he has left his notebook at the police station so he can't write any notes. Can you help him to remember what happened? Look carefully at the picture and then turn the page.

MEMORY GAME

How much can you remember?

1 Was  shaking his fist at Milko or pulling a face at him?

2 Was  stealing a bottle of milk from Milko or picking his pockets?

3 How many were there in Milko's crate?

4  had a notebook in his hand. True or false?

5 Milko looked happy to see  True or false?

ALL ABOUT CLUES!

Look at the picture clues and write the words across.

Now look at the blue squares. You will find a word going from top to bottom of the puzzle. **Clue: Mr Plod writes on this.**

FIND THE COINS

The goblins have stolen a bag of gold coins, but they dropped them as they ran off through the Dark Wood. Help Mr Plod catch the goblins and find the coins along the way.

You will need a dice, a coloured counter, a small paper bag and 25 pennies or buttons. Every time you land on a square with coins on, put the same number of pennies or buttons in your bag. If you land on a square where Mr Plod has an accident, you must empty your bag.

13 14 15 16 17 18 19 20

30 29 28 27 26 25

SCORES

15 or more coins	Brilliant!
10-14 coins	Very good
5-9 coins	Good
Fewer than 5 coins	Have another try!

ALL MUDDLED UP!

"Hello, hello, hello!" says Mr Plod. "What do we have here?"

Someone has muddled up all the letters on this signpost. Can you help

Mr Plod to sort them out?

MISCHIEVOUS MASTER TUBBY

Master Tubby is up to mischief again. He sees something resting against a wall and so he decides to borrow it. Join the dots to find out what it is.

WHAT'S THAT?

When it's dark, Mr Plod is on the look-out for anything suspicious. What do you think he's found in these pictures?

WHICH ONE IS IT?

One of these pictures is the odd one out. Which one is it?

FIND THE SIXPENCES!

The goblins have stolen eight bags of sixpences and hidden them. Can you help Mr Plod to find them all?

WHO ARE THEY?

Mr Plod keeps photographs of all the mischievous characters in Toy Town, but someone has broken into the Police Station and cut them up. Can you put the tops, middles and bottoms together?

POOR MR PLOD

While Mr Plod is talking to Mr Straw, one of the farm animals takes a sandwich from his basket. Help Mr Plod to find out which animal it is. You will have to look for clues!

THE LOST KEY

Mr Plod has lost a very important key. It's the key to his jail! Can you help him to find it?

Answers

Page 3
What's Wrong?
Noddy should have a blue hat; Master Tubby should be wearing stripy shorts, not trousers; Big Ears should be wearing a striped jersey, not a shirt and tie; Milko should be carrying pints of milk, not Mr Sparks's spanners!

Page 4
Odd One Out
The third helmet has six points on its star; the first pencil has no eraser; the second whistle has a round hole in it.

Page 5
The Dark Wood

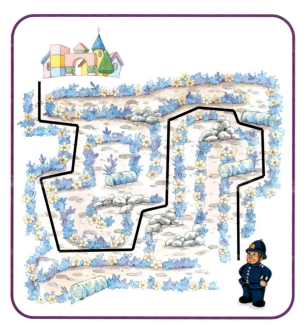

Page 6
Spot the Difference

Page 8
Who Stole the Fish?
The culprit is Sammy Sailor!

Page 10
Memory Game
1 Pulling a face 2 Stealing a bottle of milk
3 Five 4 False 5 False

Page 11
All About Clues!
Words across are NODDY, PLOD, TESSIE, BIGEARS, PLOD, SAMMY, NODDY. The word reading downwards is NOTEPAD.

Answers

Page 14
All Muddled Up!

Page 15
Mischievous Master Tubby

Master Tubby has taken a BICYCLE!

Page 16
What's That?

1 Noddy's car
2 bicycle
3 petrol pump
4 street lamp

Page 17
Which One Is It?

No. 3 is different. Mr Plod isn't holding a pencil!

Page 18
Find the Sixpences!

Page 20
Who Are They?

No. 3 goes with No. 9 and No. 6 (Gobbo)
No. 5 goes with No. 8 and No. 2 (Sammy Sailor)
No. 7 goes with No. 1 and No. 4 (Master Tubby)

Page 21
Poor Mr Plod

It's the duck! (The clues are the duck footprints next to Mr Plod's bicycle and the sandwich crumbs all around the duck.)

Page 22
The Lost Key

Silly Mr Plod. The key is still in the jail lock!